*the Institute
of Management*

The Institute of Management (IM) is the leading
organisation for professional management.
Its purpose is to promote the art and science of
management in every sector and at every level,
through research, education, training and
development, and representation of members'
views on management issues.

This series is commissioned by IM Enterprises
Limited, a subsidiary of the Institute of Management,
providing commercial services.

**Management House,
Cottingham Road,
Corby,
Northants NN17 1TT
Tel: 01536 204222;
Fax: 01536 201651
Website: http://www.inst-mgt.org.uk**

Registered in England no 3834492
Registered office: 2 Savoy Court, Strand,
London WC2R 0EZ

CONTENTS

Conflict surrounds our daily lives. Verbal conflict now quickly escalates into litigation or even physical violence. Road rage, air rage and the neighbours from hell are all symptoms of today's world. This book concentrates on the business side of this competitive environment though the lessons we will learn may also be applicable to our social life.

We start the week by examining the nature of conflict and its causes and learn that conflict is not necessarily negative. When conflict is managed constructively it can produce the stimulus to achieve a sustained competitive advantage. However, when interpersonal and interdepartmental conflict is ignored and allowed to fester it can have a devastating effect on a business.

The book will also consider the growth in business litigation and its cost to the organisation. It aims to demonstrate the value of the alternative approaches including negotiation, mediation and arbitration. But the key aim of this book is to introduce the concept of the collaborative culture involving customer, suppliers and employees in resolving conflict to the benefit of all. The week ahead comprises:

Sunday	Understanding the issues
Monday	Recognising the causes
Tuesday	An alternative to lawyers
Wednesday	Ears that hear!
Thursday	Putting it right
Friday	Working together
Saturday	The individual role

Understanding conflict

We all experience conflict in our everyday working life. It may occur on the way to work when another motorist shows their obvious dislike of us or our driving. Sometimes such an incident makes us so angry that it affects our mood for the whole day, which in turn could lead to further conflict. Or it could start with a confrontation at work with a colleague who takes issue with a position you hold or an action that you propose. In some situations whole departments or groups of people are engaged in conflict with other departments over a perceived course of action or the dispersal of scarce resources. Occasionally these confrontations may culminate in physical violence.

The nature of conflict

Some of this conflict at work is relatively easy to recognise, though, as we will see later, not necessarily easy to resolve. It can show itself through obvious enmity between individuals or in disputes between organised groups of people. Individual conflict may manifest itself in a number of ways including angry shouting, in always taking a contrary position to another person, or even in a sullen withdrawal from all interaction. A common example is the conflict that can arise between an employee and their supervisor. Interdepartmental disputes are commonplace in business but the most telling example of group conflict is a dispute between management and labour which results in a ruinous strike.

Unfortunately, much of the conflict in business is hidden and unspoken. It can pervade an organisation like a deadly cancer. We will spend time during Monday examining how hidden conflict is caused but the crucial point is that nobody is aware that an underlying conflict is affecting the business situation. As a result no action is taken to resolve the issue or even a series of issues until it is far too late to be effective.

But we also have to understand that conflict in itself is neither good nor bad. Conflict is in the nature of business. Conflict in the workplace and between businesses is the natural result of the competitive environment in which business operates. In the words of the old song, business must learn to 'eliminate the negative and accentuate the positive'.

Competition
The last century witnessed a continuous struggle between the concepts of the centrally directed economy or the free market economy. In the main this conflict of ideas has been resolved in the favour of the free market, and so we enter the new century in the environment of the global market place. In other words it is now almost universally accepted that competition (a form of conflict) is the essential driver in

achieving national and corporate economic success. We now recognise that competition spurs new ideas, new technologies, better products and a better service to customers.

Yet remnants of the defeated philosophy still survive in society and business. Corporate conflict to secure an increased market share is often extolled but the competitive urge in individuals (who make up the corporations) is often decried. The competitive individual is seen as an obstacle in developing a fair and collaborative culture. An example of this attitude can be seen in the state school system which for decades has tried to eliminate competitive sport on the altar of a collective vision. Of course the extremes of individual and corporate competition should be curbed or regulated; that is only commonsense. But we have to recognise that conflict is the natural result of people working together. In the working environment, conflict can be constructive or destructive. The trick is to manage conflict in all its forms to encourage the constructive and aim to eliminate the destructive.

Constructive conflict

Conflict is not a tangible process of business which can always be objectively described. It lies in the perceptions and minds of people who are engaged in it. However, it can become tangible when it shows itself in argument or other forms of communication. In a collaborative culture (which we discuss on Friday), constructive criticism or conflict is welcomed and encouraged. The aim of constructive conflict is to:

- resolve a problem
- resolve disagreements
- envisage new breakthroughs
- improve a product or service
- help people meet the challenge of change
- increase and widen involvement
- help create a collaborative culture.

Absence of conflict

An organisation in which there is little or no conflict is like a giant tanker adrift on the ocean without an engine or compass. Sooner or later it will run aground or strike perilous rocks. Yet to the casual visitor there is a comfortable atmosphere and the people seem content. Articles may even be written about the absence of conflict and the high standard of personnel relationships. In truth, management and people are concentrating on maintaining the status quo and in terms of the market place the company is moribund.

Nobody is arguing about tomorrow so change catches everybody by surprise. Many previously great corporations have become complacent and lethargic and have almost happily gone to their destruction.

Destructive conflict

So the healthy organisation needs conflict but if that conflict is not recognised or managed then it can become destructive. Destructive conflict will lead to a similar end as with the group without any conflict, though perhaps at an even faster pace. Conflict is destructive when it:

- obscures the real source of problems
- prevents decisions
- promotes the wrong decision for personal ends
- diverts energy from important activities or issues
- leads to a misuse of resources
- destroys the morale of employees
- divides people into warring groups
- confuses customers and suppliers
- destroys stakeholder confidence.

Bureaucracy and business
As an aside, in 1970 the government of Edward Heath wanted to promote understanding between the civil service and the leaders of business. A monthly luncheon was organised at Admiralty House at which representatives of each discipline would share opinions. The author remembers one such luncheon when the difference between both was defined as 'the civil service is organised to eliminate all

conflict from meetings while business is organised to create conflict in decision-making'.

Definition

It is now time for us to turn our attention to a workable definition for conflict and to consider the different types of conflict. The dictionary definition of conflict is, 'opposition between ideas, interest etc. which lead to controversy'. The psychologist's definition takes us a little further: 'opposition between two simultaneous but incompatible wishes or impulses, sometimes leading to emotional tension'.

The business definition which best fits the aims of this book comes from the American author, Eric Van Slyke (*Listening to Conflict*, Amacom 1998) who defines conflict as 'the competition between interdependent parties who perceive that they have incompatible needs, goals, desires or ideas'. The latter definition emphasises, as Slyke notes, three elements which are essential to our understanding of conflict in business, namely:

- Competition
- Interdependence
- Perception.

Competition

We touched on the broad concept of competition earlier but there are many types of competition within an organisation which we need to consider. The company as a whole may be competing with other companies to win market share but the individuals within the company may well have individual competitive goals.

Within strong individuals the competitive urge is with themselves. They set themselves objectives which they strive to meet, sometimes to obsessive levels. It may be a simple objective such as reducing their golf handicap which affects no one except perhaps their long suffering families. But for many it will be a business objective to reach a certain salary level or position by a given age or date, which could have a profound effect on others.

This type of competition can be aggressive or passive. The individual may be totally directed to prevent another person achieving those objectives. If this energy is directed totally at the personal goal with little reference to the corporate or collaborative goals it will have a disruptive effect on the organisation. But if the individual could be convinced that their personal goals are more likely to be achieved if the corporate objectives are met, then that energy will play a positive role.

At a lower level but equally disruptive is the personal competition of 'winning' over colleagues or others. This form of competition is not always conscious and is often exhibited by people with low self-confidence. The outward signs are stubbornness, a refusal to participate or even bouts of bad temper. This form of competitiveness can be damaging to building a team environment, in tackling a difficult task or in attempting to resolve a problem.

Interpersonal competition can arise in many ways, which will become clear when we examine the causes of conflict on

Monday. We should also recognise that teams or whole departments may exhibit similar competitive traits within the organisation. In some cases this will stem naturally from the company's competitive environment but it may also be a symptom of the influence of a strong leader with a highly developed competitive streak.

The most important lesson to be learned is that competition and thus conflict are natural in a healthy striving organisation. It is a powerful energy source which needs to be channelled properly to release the full potential of the organisation.

Interdependence

Understanding the interdependent relationships and dependencies in an organisation lies at the heart of conflict resolution. In business few individuals can really act alone. Whatever our level in the organisation we are dependant on other people taking action if we are to achieve our own company goals or even our personal goals. We have to work together with many other people in a vast interdependent maze and will sometimes feel like a very small cog in a big wheel. This can be both frustrating and the source of much interpersonal conflict, not least because we are not able to act interdependently and 'do it our way'.

Consider the possible points of conflict for the individual or groups of people in the following typical scenario. The role of the manager is to develop, allocate and explain the tasks and goals to subordinates and then to provide the equipment and resources needed. The worker is now dependant on a supplier (inside or outside the organisation) to provide partly worked product, material or information in a timely fashion to the right standards. The worker's role is to complete the task entrusted to them and pass on their finished work to a customer (again inside or outside the organisation) in the quantity, to the quality and at the time required. This simple process will be reflected hundreds of times throughout every organisation. Each of the points highlighted could be the source of problems which have to be resolved. This is not a new concept; it is called 'process management'.

Perception

Our definition stated that incompatible needs, goals, desires or ideas are the principle elements in conflict at work. However, we were also careful to qualify that statement with the word 'perceived'. People's perceptions play a large part in conflict and in making it difficult to resolve. Perceptions are very personal and relate to training, experience and behavioural attitudes which have been forged over a period of time in both work and social interaction. We have to recognise that in any dispute several sets of perceptions or even prejudices may be in play.

Perception is not confined to the subjective elements of an issue. For example people's perception of 'on time' may well differ. An objective requirement for goods to be delivered at 10am would appear to be clear and unequivocal, but not to everybody. Some people, recognising the variability of traffic etc. would happily accept a tolerance of say an hour each side; for them the requirement is now 'somewhere' between 9am and 11am. Remember the application of the citizen's charter by British Rail? They promised a high percentage of trains would arrive 'on time' and defined that as plus or minus five minutes. When they had difficulty in keeping their promise they decided to change the standard to plus or minus fifteen minutes rather than aiming for improvement.

We will look at perception again, in particular when we look at the techniques for resolving conflict on Thursday.

Summary

We have spent Sunday developing our understanding of the nature of conflict and its impact on the workplace. We have recognised that conflict is a natural corollary to the competitive environment in which business operates. Perhaps the most important idea we have considered is that conflict is vital to the health and success of every organisation – that positive attitude enables us to face both the constructive and the destructive elements of conflict. We now realise that conflict needs to be managed if we are to gain the advantages of constructive conflict. At the same time we are aware of the elements of conflict that must be considered if we are to eliminate destructive conflict. They include the interdependent nature of work processes and the power of perception.

Our work today can be summarised as recognising:

- that conflict at work is with collegues
- that conflict can be overt or hidden
- that conflict can be good or bad
- that competition is natural
- that conflict can be individual or in groups
- that perceptions play a part in conflict.

On Monday we will develop our understanding by examining the causes of conflict.

Causes of conflict

Diversity in people, processes, communication and management causes most conflict in business. The role of management is crucial. Strong management provides a sense of purpose and confidence which encourages constructive conflict. Weak management breeds uncertainty and low morale which is at the root of destructive conflict. Today we are going to examine the differences in:

- the behaviour of people
- the variation in process
- the use of communication
- the management of diversity.

MORNING JONES   MORNING STEVENS

The behaviour of people

Just because people work together in the same team or department does not mean that they will get along with each other or that they will agree to the same actions in specific situations. Unfortunately, there are as many differences in people as there are people, but in the workplace each individual will tend to behave in a recognisable style. A number of factors will determine that style and they can be summarised as follows:

- personality
- values
- expectations
- attitude
- needs
- perceptions.

Personality
We tend to make our early judgements about people on the basis of our perception of their personality. Clearly there are people with incredible personality or charisma who will dominate any group they are part of or join, but they are a small minority. Nevertheless there is a sufficient difference in the span of personalities to create tension and strong likes and dislikes. The adjectives we use indicate the graduations and the challenge to create synergy in a team; at one end we have 'aggressive', 'forceful' and 'strong'; at the other end are 'weak', 'timid' and 'easy to get on with'. These descriptions also make it clear that personalities can change to meet different situations.

Attitude
Attitude is closely linked to personality and is most easily

recognised in personal style. At one extreme the personal attitude to an issue will be wholly dominated by the achievement of a personal goal. At the other end of the spectrum, individuals can be wholly dominated by a concern for people. These wide differences in attitude can be a source for strong conflict. We shall consider the Mouton-Blake Grid which examines this area on Wednesday.

Values
People at work exhibit diverse cultural and/or religious values which are not necessarily shared by their colleagues. People make judgements based on their values so when issues arise that involve those values there is an opportunity for conflict. We have all witnessed the severe conflict often culminating in violence that can arise from differing ethnic values.

Needs
Different people have different needs or levels of satisfaction and when those needs are not satisfied, it can cause frustration and conflict.

Expectations
Expectations can go beyond needs and most people expect and plan for outcomes. If these expectations are not met it can cause conflict.

Perceptions
We do not all view the world from the same perspective. As a result we have different perceptions of how a job should be carried out or how a problem arises. People do interpret the same data in different ways and so conflict can result. Individual perceptions are particularly strong where there is a lack of purpose or requirements are not clearly defined and agreed.

Variation in processes

There is variation in all our processes but if variation is
measured, and the process remains in control, work will be
carried out in a non-stressful environment without conflict.
At this stage it may be useful to instigate conflict to consider
how the stable process could be enhanced. However, for
many people this would be a luxury. The normal situation
which results from a lack of clarity adds variation upon
variation. As a result each work situation is centred around
disagreements about:

- facts
- methods
- goals
- resources.

Facts
Sometimes people only hear the facts that they want to hear.
They ignore important relevant facts as they proceed and
sooner or later are in conflict with colleagues or even
customers. On the other hand different individuals may have
different definitions of the process or, more often, inadequate
rather than wrong information. Some individuals on the
team may have access to external facts that appear to
contradict the understanding of the team. Facts can also be
distorted in their recording and in communication.
Frustrated managers can be heard shouting, 'Give me the
truth, not the facts'.

Goals
Too often goals are set in isolation from the processes of
work and without reference to other interested parties. The
result is groups of people driving goals which are directly in

opposition to goals for people in another department. For example, if the purchasing department has been set up with its principal goal being to 'save money' it will soon be in conflict with the producing department whose goal is 'world class quality'. But sometimes the conflict about goals comes about because no goals have been set and every department is working to changing desires. We will be looking at the vital part collaborative goals can play in a successful business culture on Friday.

Methods

Disagreement about the methods to be used in a process are a source of continuous conflict. There are always people who insist on doing it 'my way' but in the main dispute about procedures and methods is due to weak management. Too many people are expected to learn what to do by haphazard methods or from people next to them. The new era of the *knowledge worker* is more likely to exacerbate this issue rather than eliminate it as many claim. An organisation of independent people all doing their 'own thing' could be

exciting but if it is not linked by a collaborative culture it is merely divisive.

Resources
When resources are scarce or do not live up to expectations the competition can become fierce. Facts, goals and methods are all manipulated to secure the best possible deal.

Use of communication

Everyone at work is involved in communication in some form or another. We talk and write to our customers and suppliers and sometimes actually listen to them. We also communicate in many ways with our colleagues, and with a multitude of people in other organisations on whom we depend for our ultimate success. If any of these communication channels break down, or our messages are misunderstood, we risk disruption and conflict.

Current management practices inhibit clear, concise and direct communication of the information needed to get things done successfully. Some of them create barriers to communication between each level of management as well as between departmental peers at each level. Each of these barriers are a source of conflict or hurdles to be overcome. The major barriers to communication are so crucial to the resolution of conflict that they are worth summarising here as:

- specialisation (or departmental fortresses)
- the division between thinkers and doers
- tradition and culture
- emotions at work

- lack of a common language
- corporate chateaux.

Specialisation and departmental fortresses
Major work processes or work activities are divided into a host of specialised activities. The process of *specialisation* has made modern business possible but it has also created problems which lead to conflict. The steady division of business operations has led to a horizontal division between departments and a vertical division between management and people. Over time each division has created barriers both to communication and to an understanding of how the business is operating. The phenomenon of *'them and us'* is much broader than the division between managers and workers.

Organisations manage people and work through functional departments. The managers and people within these departments communicate well with each other but are dedicated only to their own specific goals. Often their objectives are divisive so that departments compete, rather than collaborate, with each other. This traditional system has created 'departmental fortresses' across the organisation. Ultimately in this environment, an organisation sees its customers and suppliers as combatants to be overcome.

The division between thinkers and doers
The major elements of the style of management based on specialisation were command, control and compliance. Jobs were designed so that each worker had one highly repetitive task, and jobs that required many skills were replaced by narrowly defined jobs in which supervisors made all the decisions. The worker didn't have to think: he or she just had to be controlled. This division between the *thinkers* and the *doers* has persisted to this day. Yet in modern industry, the repetitive non-thinking jobs are being eliminated or carried out by machines and workers are thus being asked to return to a multi-skilled thinking process in work; in today's jargon, they are being '*empowered*'. Unfortunately, however, the traditional controlling instincts of management remain as another source of conflict.

Tradition and culture
There are hidden barriers to communication based on individual perceptions of tradition, culture and status. Individuals will formulate or interpret a message according to their own perception of 'what goes on around here' or 'what they *really* meant'. A long tradition of authoritarian messages from on-high will establish a cynical mistrust of all management communications because the intended recipients 'turn off' and do not listen to the message.

Emotions at work

The traditional, rational world of business believes that our emotions are better kept private. This is a dangerous attitude as, like it or not, human feelings affect every job and organisation. Too often at work we try to stifle our feelings, and yet, even in a business environment, our emotional needs can be harnessed for positive interaction and positive results. Hidden or bottled-up emotions can lead to frustration and destructive conflict.

Lack of a common language

An area of language difficulty in business communication that is not so readily recognised is the different language used by executives, management and workers. Executives are reputed to be concerned about only three issues: (i) making money, (ii) not losing money, and (iii) money!

Although this is perhaps not totally fair, it does serve to illustrate a serious issue in internal business communications. Workers on their part do not talk in the language of money, but instead in the language of things and getting things done. They may be interested in the worth of their pay packet, but they are not much concerned with revenue and profit ratios. Yet too often executives will talk to their workers in the language of business finance and assume that the latter should know what is happening. Middle managers are caught in between as they attempt to talk both languages and often just end up confusing everybody. This was a common area of conflict in the days of labour unrest and strikes.

Corporate chateaux

As the channels of communication and action became more

complex and time-consuming, the thinkers needed people
to advise them and to help control the disparate elements of
the business. These advisors are organised into staff groups
who exercise power and control on behalf of executives.
Their 'customer' is senior management rather than the
actual customer of the business. As the eyes, ears and voice
of management, they serve to reinforce the separation
between management and worker. Even more important,
this trend has divided management both from
communication with the customer and the real issues of the
marketplace.

In most businesses today, a substantial proportion of
managers and employees have little or no contact with the
customer or with the people who make products or deliver
services. They live in *corporate chateaux* (like the generals in
the Great War) and spend their working hours with other
managers or 'members of staff'. They are far removed from
changing customer perceptions, the 'insignificant' problems
of workers and 'difficult' customers. Too often, their energy
is expended on jockeying for political position and
extending their own privileges rather than on improving the
business.

Management of diversity

Management and the system they use cause disruptive
conflict in many businesses. Many of their decisions appear
to be based on subjective or hidden agendas. Also, because in
general managers do not like conflict, they take actions to
stifle conflict or disagreement which can easily lead to
frustration.

Typical management behaviour patterns that add to uncertainty and disagreement can be summarised as:

- surrounding themselves with individuals who 'think my way' and are 'one of us'
- always settling for compromise to avoid strong disagreements
- playing the team loyalty card so that disagreement appears traitorous
- disparate treatment in the administration of discipline
- employing an uneven or unfair reward and recognition system in order to divide and rule
- ignoring or hiding serious differences in a group so that the operation appears to be acting in unison and, therefore, to be well managed
- setting rather than discussing and agreeing goals with subordinates
- avoiding all risk of conflict with peers to the extent that interdepartmental problems are not addressed

- leaving parties to disagreement unclear as to decisions so that the conflict is resumed at every opportunity
- having clear favourites or cronies and encouraging division
- rarely setting a clear sense of purpose or direction or 'taking a stand' on any issue.

Summary

Today we have looked at a series of causes of conflict within the daily working environment. We have noted that some conflict is good but in the main we have concentrated on the causes of disruptive conflict. One of the most important issues we raised during Monday was the crucial role played by management in the cause of conflict. Over the week we will examine positive actions to resolve conflict. Tomorrow, Tuesday, we will focus on litigation and the place of ADR (alternative dispute resolution).

Perils of litigation

Perhaps the most pernicious trend in business over recent decades has been the increasing influence of the lawyers and the corporate legal department. The businessman's reaction to a newsflash stating that six hundred lawyers are feared drowned in a cruise ship disaster – 'Sounds like a good start to me' – may be a joke but it is a natural reaction. The real point of the joke is that such macabre humour works because it expresses a shared truth. But to provide a sense of scale to this issue there are now more attorneys in the United States than in the rest of the world put together. Western Europe now appears to want to play catch-up.

Lawyers have no role to play in the essential processes of business, yet our corporations are dominated by them. We have now reached a position where it now seems impossible to have any meaningful business meeting or negotiation without the presence of lawyers. But that was not the environment in which business was conducted in earlier years, including those periods of explosive and successful business growth in the latter part of the 19th century. In the main, business leaders discussed the pertinent issues on their marketing, operational and funding constraints. They reached agreement and then *instructed* their lawyers to draw up contracts based on that agreement. Most of the enduring business giants were founded on that basis.

Too often today, the all-pervading presence of the legal eagle obfuscates the simple principles of business. The successful deal used to be one that was good for both parties; now it appears to be one that steals a legal march on the other party.

From a business perspective, there is an interesting aspect in the position of the law relative to the normal business relationship between customer and supplier. In less than thirty years, that relative position has been almost completely reversed. In this area, common or case law was based primarily on the concept of *caveat emptor*, or 'let the buyer beware'. But since the advent of global competition and consumer power, the perception of the customer and the law has had to change. The consumer is now organised and wields political clout. The legislature has responded with a host of consumer oriented legislation. This trend has now been combined with the formation of many new regulatory bodies and quasi-political pressure groups ever eager to constrain business. The legal basis for the key relationship is now 'let the seller beware'. This volte-face is not necessarily wrong, but has resulted in a different business environment.

On another front, the deregulated and fee conscious lawyer can encourage consumers, business associates, employees, and every conceivable environmental group to find legal precedents with which to further lambast business. Harassment, stress and trauma are having expensive legal implications. As a result business is seeking to protect itself with more lawyers, fine print and legal jargon to avoid the perils of litigation.

Cost of litigation

All of this activity is adding horrendous cost to the operation of business and public sector organisation. This is illustrated in three sectors as in:

- the high costs of legal advice both internal and external to the organisation
- the constant risk of punitive damages
- the diversion of focus from the key processes and the purpose of the organisation.

There is another aspect of litigation that concerns industry, commerce and public sector organisations. There are few winners and it is rare for either litigant in legal conflict to gain total satisfaction. The wasted time and costs, the mud thrown in public and the loss of market credibility are common to both sides of the dispute. Too much, too long and too costly is the business view of litigation.

All of these factors have brought about a reaction. Increasingly companies are seeking an alternative to court room disputes. Negotiation, mediation and arbitration are now coming to the fore as the preferred early response to conflict in many organisations. In the United States it has now become a mainstream activity with the title ADR or 'alternative dispute resolution'. We will spend most of the rest of today considering ADR.

Alternative dispute resolution

Alternative dispute resolution (ADR) is an all-embracing term used to describe alternative methods, other than formal court litigation, to resolve a dispute or conflict. ADR methods used to resolve conflicts include negotiation, mediation and arbitration and a number of derivatives from these three approaches. The term is widely used in the United States but in Europe the elements tend to be used separately.

To aid understanding of the ramifications of ADR we will consider the subject under the following headings:

- Background and origins
- Typical users
- Advantages and disadvantages
- Alternative elements
- Binding or non-binding
- When to use ADR.

Background and origins

There is nothing new in the concept of ADR. Throughout history people have turned to arbitration or mediation from 'wise men' rather than resort to the courts. Many highly organised religious and ethnic sects defined sophisticed and binding arbitration procedures for internal disputes. Their lead has been followed by trade and professional organisations. For example, few doctors or lawyers in Britain would dare oppose a decision by the British Medical Association (BMA) or the Law Society. As we noted earlier, the founders of the great corporations in the nineteenth century rarely resorted to the courts on issues that mattered to them.

The present term ADR began in the United States and became institutionalised as long ago as 1922, when business leaders established the Arbitration Society of America. This became the prime lobbying force in amending USA interstate law and many commercial rules or standards for arbitration. Since then the key force in championing ADR has been the American Arbitration Association (AAA) which has promoted the development of out of court techniques in a wide range of areas. These include family controversies, warranty claims, patent disputes, building design and construction issues and a series of public service areas of dispute. For a long time in the USA the leading users of ADR were the state and federal agencies. More recently industry and commerce have increasingly turned to ADR methods.

Typical users

The conversion to ADR in the USA was heralded in 1976 when the Chief Justice of the Supreme Court, Warren E. Burger, expressed his concern about the irrelevance of the legal system to the real problems of the nation:

> 'We may well be on our way to a society overrun by lawyers, hungry as locusts, and brigades of judges in numbers never before contemplated. We have reached the point where our system of justice (both state and federal) may literally break down before the end of the century'.

This prophetic statement had an immediate effect on the agencies of government but it took until well into the nineties before American business turned to ADR. In most business innovations the USA tends to lead the world by a number of years but in this arena experience across the Atlantic appears to be similar. The lead industries to recognise the value of ADR solutions have been the construction, chemical, pharmaceutical and the defence industries in both Europe and the USA. All are project oriented businesses with high risk opportunities for expensive litigation.

There are signs that the financial and banking world are turning towards ADR with the prime movers coming from the insurance industry. The effort expended in the insurance field to settle millions of relatively minor claims has led to the adoption of negotiation rather than confrontation as the preferred method.

Across all industry the most extensive use of ADR has been in the area of manager versus labour disputes. Since the Thatcher era brought clarity and focus to industrial disputes, both management and labour have turned to variants of ADR for the settlement of disputes. Nearly all labour and unionised contracts have some form of binding dispute resolution incorporated in the agreements. Britain, once typified by its level of industrial dispute, now vies with the USA in its ability to manage disagreement short of conflict. Steadily this internal experience will influence companies to turn in the same direction for the resolution of external conflict. In time this movement will bring about a new collaborative culture, an idea we will develop on Friday.

The advantages of ADR
The advantage of ADR versus the formal litigation process can be summarised as follows:

- it takes less time to resolve a conflict from the beginning to the end
- it costs less because of legal fees, employee time away from work and lower court costs
- parties to the dispute can select an arbitrator or facilitator with specific industry knowledge rather than having to rely on randomly selected legal judges
- parties to the dispute can control the venue and the time frame for negotiation rather than having to fit the courtroom and the court calendar
- the non-adversarial nature of ADR makes it easier to maintain relationships with the opponent after the issue has been resolved
- the process is more confidential than litigation and court reporters where the arguments become public record
- the process is more flexible without the necessity to follow court procedures and the rules of evidence.

The disadvantages of ADR

Depending on circumstances there could be drawbacks to using ADR methods. These can be summarised as follows:

- the longer timeframe involved in litigation may suit one litigant for financial or other reasons
- court rules could force the disclosure of information on the public record to the advantage of one of the disputants
- if the law surrounding the issue appears to be favourable to one party's side, they are likely to favour litigation
- ADR settlements do not set legal precedents as in a court of law. If in the nature of the dispute one party envisages many similar cases will arise they might value the setting of precedents

- it may be to the advantage of one party to make the result of litigation public, for example to discourage a rash of minor cases which create irritating diversions of focus
- in complex situations or in cases with say 'international' reverberations some litigants might feel more comfortable with the clarity and precedence of a court case.

In general ADR seems to work best with companies of a similar size and operating in similar business environments. Smaller companies or individuals often feel overawed or perhaps that they lack the negotiating clout to take on the large corporation in ADR. For them the courtroom represents a level playing field.

Alternative elements of ADR

There are principal elements of ADR and a number of variants which in some cases act as a kind of 'halfway house' between ADR and litigation. They can be summarised as follows:

- Negotiation
- Conciliation
- Mediation
- Arbitration
- Mediation/arbitration
- Transformative mediation
- Mini-trial
- Private judging
- Summary jury trial.

Negotiation is a process by which the disputants discuss their differences and move toward a settlement that is acceptable to all parties. It is the least costly resolution technique because the parties themselves control the process and voluntarily reach a solution. There are two principal strategies to obtain the desired outcome from negotiation: *competitive* and *collaborative*. In competitive negotiation, one party seeks to maximise its own gain, generally at the expense of the other party. In collaborative negotiation, the approach is oriented toward a mutually equitable solution often described as the 'win-win' solution. We will return to negotiation on Thursday.

Conciliation is a variation of negotiation in which a third party is used to bring the contestants together. Although the communication pattern may at times resemble negotiation, the conciliator does not take an active role in the negotiations. The conciliator's role is helping the combatants limit and control their emotions and negative rhetoric. Conciliation is a constructive and facilitated form of negotiation.

Mediation is a structured and voluntary problem solving process. An impartial third party is engaged by the disputants to assist them in directly negotiating their own solution to the decision or to solve the problem for them. The role of the mediator is to facilitate discussion, solicit honest evaluation of the dispute and to foster a collaborative atmosphere. The key to the success of mediation is the ability of the mediator to engender trust so that the parties will confide in him or her.

Arbitration is the best known and the most formalised

alternative to a formal court trial. It is a process in which the parties submit their dispute to a neutral third person or arbitrator for decision. The arbitrator is usually an expert in the area of dispute and is chosen by the parties on the basis of their experience. Their decisions are usually binding on both parties unless there has been agreement otherwise. Arbitration is very much like court deliberation. Usually the parties are represented by legal counsel or some other individual with relevant expertise. In many industries and professional bodies, individual companies or parties to a contract agree, as part of the contract, to abide by arbitration of any disputes that might arise.

Mediation/arbitration is a two-step process designed to bring the benefits of both mediation and arbitration together in resolving a dispute. Arbitration is deferred until mediation reaches an impasse and appears to be unsuccessful. If this occurs the mediator calls a halt and informs both parties of the decision to proceed to arbitration. The arbitrator will hear the presentation of both parties and then make an award or decision. Parties can appeal the arbitrator's award or decision but they now move to full litigation. This process relies strongly on the parties' trust in the mediator.

Transformative mediation is a recent addition to ADR techniques. This practice puts its emphasis on the process of mediation rather than the result. It is used in social service and family situations and has been utilised as a training exercise for corporations searching for a corporate culture.

Mini-trial is a structured settlement process designed to bring the focus of disputing parties into a final decision generally made by a panel of senior executives from the disputing organisations, who are not personally involved with the dispute. Mini-trials are voluntary and non-binding. The parties have no obligation to settle through the executives. However, this technique has proved very successful in resolving high profile commercial and business disputes, particularly when the relationship of the parties must be maintained after the dispute is resolved. It allows the parties to maintain privacy, control litigation costs and avoid harming their relationship.

Private judging is a process in which the contestants engage a neutral third party, such as a lawyer or non-legal expert, to perform as judge or referee. The proceedings are identical to trial proceedings, and the rules of evidence are enforced. A major advantage of private judging is that the case is not subject to the court calendar. This process is quick and efficient but it can be very expensive.

Summary jury trial lawyers for the respective parties present a brief synopsis of their case to a jury that, after deliberation, makes a non-binding advisory decision. It is a court supervised proceeding whose purpose is to provide the parties with a 'simulated verdict' and a sense of how a typical jury might rule. The advisory decision is often powerful enough to break any deadlock in negotiations. A party who is dissatisfied with the verdict may reject it and proceed to a normal trial.

Binding or non-binding

ADR has two approaches to resolving conflict: binding and non-binding. In most instances negotiation, conciliation and mediation are non-binding unless the parties enter into some kind of binding agreement before commencing the process.

The usual approach is that when the parties have reached agreement it is registered as a binding contractual agreement in writing.

On the other hand, arbitration, mini-trials and private judging are far more formal, and the parties often provide for a binding agreement before initiating ADR. Then if agreement is made at the time of settlement the parties are precluded from additional adjudication unless the agreement is obtained by fraud or technical or legal deficiency exists. When binding written agreements have been challenged or ignored the courts will generally enforce the agreement.

When to use ADR

American arbitration associations advise that ADR should be the chosen method for any or all of the following reasons:

- to avoid the win-lose outcome
- when lawsuits could endanger long-term relationships
- when court decisions resolve the legal issues but not the underlying cause
- when long-term litigation will be severely disruptive to the business
- when both parties want a simple way to resolve disputes
- when the cost of litigation is prohibitive or will exceed the damages involved
- if there is no need to establish a precedent
- where privacy is essential.

- where fairness and justice will be best obtained by using ADR.

Summary

Today we started by considering the growing expense and disruption involved in turning to litigation as the prime method for resolving conflict. But the main area we examined was the alternative dispute resolution movement in the USA. Clearly ADR is a good way to resolve conflict and presents alternatives to litigation that are potentially far less costly and ultimately more satisfactory. Though the ADR movement is American the main elements of negotiation, mediation and arbitration are well proven and available in the UK.

Tomorrow we concern ourselves with the prime skill needed in dispute resolution, that is listening.

The power of listening

On Tuesday in discussing litigation we were concentrating on inter-organisational conflict. However, in the workplace the principal concern in the elimination of disruptive conflict is interpersonal conflict. Managers and personnel officers are often involved in mediating disputes between employees, colleagues, customers and suppliers on an individual basis. One skill above all is essential to resolving personal conflict, namely listening.

In his powerful book *Listening to Conflict* (Amacom 1998), Erik Van Syke argues that listening is the key to constructive conflict resolution. He notes that 'the problem in conflict, however, is not whether the other party listens to us, but rather whether we listen to and understand the other party's perspective. Only after we have listened to the other party will that party listen to us'.

When we begin the resolution process by listening, we create an environment that demonstrates a desire for constructive resolution. It reduces the chance of personality differences which will interfere with constructive problem solving. But we cannot listen to and understand others until we know how to listen to and understand ourselves.

So the shape of Wednesday breaks down quite easily into four main segments as follows:

- listening to ourselves
- listening to others
- analysing what we hear
- obstacles to be overcome.

Listening to ourselves

If we do not listen to and make some attempt to understand ourselves we are unlikely to be able to hear and comprehend other people's reaction to us. All of us are a mixture of attitudes, feelings and emotions stemming from our background, experience and basic personality. In many people this will also create prejudices which may or not be recognised by the individual concerned. As we saw on Monday each of these distinct differences provide an opportunity for interpersonal friction which can lead to conflict. The more we become aware of our own distinct attitudes or operating style the more we will learn to interact with others in the workplace in a positive vein.

Self-awareness allows us to see the conflict from a different perspective and then to determine how to change, or not, our actions and feelings.

Self-awareness
An organisation can ensure that its leading managers

develop a high level of self-awareness which in turn will influence other managers and employees. The author recalls that the most formative management development course that he ever attended in his business career was directed at self-awareness. His company Honeywell sent selected managers on a Mouton-Blake grid course run by an organisation called Scientific Methods Inc. The course took place over the course of a week and the twenty four participants came from a mix of leading corporations active in the UK in the early seventies.

The course week involved exercises in team collaboration, in evaluation of individual behavioural styles and in competitive conflict with other teams. The course was based on the managerial grid (see over the page) developed by Dr Robert Blake and Dr Jane Mouton who were business gurus of the period.

The contention was that individuals exhibit a dominant style in their approach to business and their interaction with others. Perhaps of more interest was that when an individual was unable to achieve their objective in their dominant style they resorted to a back-up style.

The range of styles was determined by the grid axis. One axis was based on a high concern for people and the other on a high concern for production or meeting the objective. So for an example a person with a driving concern to achieving objectives but with little concern for people would be evaluated as a 9.1 style. Typically a 9.1 dominant style would opt out or exhibit a 1.1 style when the situation is not going their way. The out and out compromiser would have a 5.5 style. At no time was 9.9 projected as a target.

The Leadership Grid®

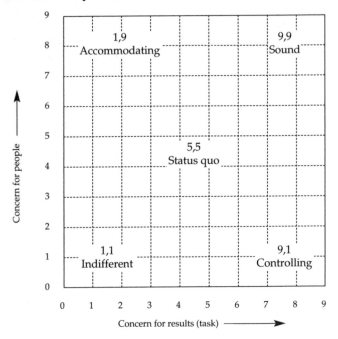

The horizontal axis represents the level of concern for obtaining results, with the term 'results' meaning such things as immediate or long-term goals, productivity or achieving the task.

The vertical axis represents the level of concern for the people involved, including the degree to which a person considers how his or her actions affect others.

Individual Grid styles

The Grid allows us to identify seven distinct styles as the

concern for people and the concern for results interact.

1.1 Indifferent – *Evade and elude*
The key word is neutral. This person goes through the motions of work, doing enough to get by, but rarely attempting to do more.

9,2 Controlling – *Direct and dominate*
The high concern for results present in this style produces determination, focus and a drive for success. This person is usually well organised, highly trained and has both the confidence to demand high standards and the courage to take calculated risks in order to achieve them. However, a low concern for people limits his or her ability to involve others and the result is a rather forceful approach.

1,9 Accommodating – *Yield and support*
The high concern for people is a valuable aid to building teams and establishing relationships. This individual maintains a heightened awareness of the feelings, goals and ambitions of others and the effect that his or her actions will have on them. He or she is approachable, friendly and always ready to listen with sympathy and encouragement. However, the low concern for results tends to shift the focus away from task achievement.

5,5 Status Quo – *Balance and compromise*
The 5,5 person avoids showing particular concern for either people or results and ends up balancing the needs of people and the achievement of results through compromise and trade-offs. The style is characterised by the attitude that "Good enough or a little better is okay'.

9,9 Sound – *Contribute and commit*
The 9,9 style is firmly based on logical reasoning and
common sense: 'If you have a problem get it out into the
open and work through it'. This person is objective and not
afraid to tackle difficult issues in an open and honest way.
The 9,9 approach gives strength and focus to a team and has
the potential resistance. Despite being effective, the style can
come across as blunt and forceful in origanisations where the
culture involves playing politics, smoothing over conflict and
deferring to authority. Given time, the 9,9 style is usually
accepted and its potential for achievement realised.

Paternalistic – *Prescribe and guide*
The Paternalistic style results from two separate Grid styles
coming together. The relationship between the 'paternalist'
and the people he or she works with is like that between
parent and child where **reward** comes from the 1,9 desire to
nurture, and **punishment** comes from the 9,1 desire to dictate
behaviour. The result is a person who commands action and
achieves results by guidance, praise, reward and subtle
punishment.

Opportunistic – *Exploit and manipulate*
The 'opportunist' approaches every situation with the
underlying attitude 'What's in it for me?' and then takes on
whatever style is most likely to provide the advantages they
seek. Opportunists shift their concerns about as needed to
create a convincing facade. They might appear strong and
capable of leading in one situation, vulnerable and in need of
guidance in another. Everything depends on the situation,
the people involved and the potential for personal gain they
perceive.

Grid styles and self-awareness

The style profiles, described above and set out diagrammatically below, are designed to help you to 'find yourself' on the Grid. Deciding what you would regard as the most suitable behaviour, and comparing this with your actual behaviour, can be a salutary exercise. It also provides a powerful incentive to establish higher standards and develop the skills needed to achieve them.

THE LEADERSHIP GRID®

Where do you fit in?

9,1 Grid Style: CONTROLLING
(Direct and Dominate)

I expect results and take control by clearly stating a course of action. I enforce rules that sustain good results and do not permit deviation.

1,9 Grid Style: ACCOMMODATING
(Yield and Comply)

I support results that establish and reinforce harmony. I generate enthusiasm by focusing on positive and pleasing aspects of work.

5,5 Grid Style: STATUS QUO
(Balance and Compromise)

I endorse results that are popular but caution against taking unnecessary risk. I test my opinions with others involved to assure ongoing acceptability.

1,1 Grid Style: INDIFFERENT
(Evade and elude)

I distance myself from taking active responsibility for results to avoid getting entangled in problems. If forced, I take a passive or supportive position.

9,9 Grid Style: SOUND
(Contribute and Commit)

I initiate team action in a way that invites involvement and commitment. I explore all facts and alternative views to reach a shared understanding of the best solution.

PATERNALISTIC Grid Style
(Prescribe and Guide)

I provide leadership by defining initiatives for myself and others. I offer praise and appreciation for support and discourage challenges to my thinking.

OPPORTUNISTIC Grid Style
(Exploit and Manipulate)

I persuade others to support results that offer me private benefit. If they themselves benefit, that is even better because it helps me gain their further support. I rely on whatever approach is needed to secure advantage.

Source:

The Leadership Grid® from *Leadership Dilemmas – Grid Solutions*, by Robert R Blake and Anne Adams McCanse (Formerly the Management Grid by Robert R Blake and Jane S Mouton), Houston, Gulf Publishing Company. Copyright 1991 by Scientific Methods, Inc. Reproduced by permission of the owners.

The objective of the course was for the individual to leave with a clear self-awareness of their own style. The course member went through a traumatic experience on the last day of the course. They had to remain silent while their colleagues evaluated their style on the grid, in their presence.

The final day assessment of style was based on a series of assessments during the week of behavioural patterns exhibited in exercises in the following areas:

- decisions
- conflict
- humour
- convictions
- emotions
- effort.

For the interest of the reader the entire course was a salutary lesson for the author. Before attending the course he believed that his success to date was his ability to get the best out of people because of a high concern for people. The course participants evaluated his dominant style as 9.1 though after a period he resorted to a 9.9 style and occasionally a 5.5 style. In other words he finally resorted to the style that would have been the most likely to bring success from the outset.

So specialist training can play a valuable part in developing self-awareness to help manage conflict. But of course self-awareness is a continuous process of listening and watching. When you know yourself as you are it enables you to have greater confidence in your ability to apply the principles of interaction required for constructive resolution of conflict.

Listening to others

We have seen that self-awareness brings self-confidence which in itself helps us to relax and listen carefully to what others have to say. Our goal is to reach a mutually satisfactory resolution of an issue. Listening helps provide us with the information we need to better understand the situation from the other party's point of view. Listening to the other side of the argument creates an environment which encourages constructive conflict and helps to defuse the destructive elements.

When another person speaks, according to Erik Van Slyke, we listen at one of six levels, namely:

- level one – passive
- level two – responsive
- level three – selective
- level four – attentive
- level five – active
- level six – emphatic.

Passive listening occurs when we consider that we are listening but in reality our mind is generally on something else. We hear the odd word, which may or not be significant, and come to a conclusion on flimsy information.

Responsive listening is similar to passive listening in that our minds are really elsewhere but we give the other person the impression that we are attentive to them by a series of verbal or non-verbal responses such as a nod or smile. We have all met the embarrassment when the response did not meet what had been said.

Selective listening means that our mind is engaged but only for short selected periods. We are listening for some indication that the speaker is in support of our argument and instantly begin planning in our mind a response or opportunity to interrupt. Instead of listening to their point of view we are listening for echoes of our viewpoint. This is a typical 9.1 management style.

Attentive listening is the most involved of the first four levels of listening which are the most commonly used levels in general business communication. It is probing and, to some extent, analytical but it is still based on the listener's agenda. We are still focused on finding a solution to conflict that suits ourselves rather than both parties.

Active listening takes listening up to the level at which we are attempting to understand the meaning that lies behind the surface. Now we are listening to more than just the words and are also engaging our eyes. We are taking note of the tone of voice, emphasis and the body gestures or expressions of the speaker. Now response is not a subterfuge to look interested but a real desire to ensure understanding.

Emphatic listening is listening with the intent to understand the other person's point of view. Empathy entails imaginatively entering into another person's feelings. It is a quality exhibited by the marketeers and salesmen often described as 'walking in the customer's shoes'. The personality is separated from the problem at the centre of the conflict; in other words one likes the person despite the conflict.

Analysing what we hear

All the listening in the world will be of little use if we are unable to use the information we have gathered. We also need to put all this listening into context. Managers and employees need to develop the skills of problem solving and process management which help provide a framework for organising information about our work. These skills also aid listening and establish the questions needed to probe deeper into the issues. Two other books in this series develop these

areas in more detail than we have room for in this book –
Successful Communication at Work and *Understanding Total Quality Management.*

Some obstacles to listening

We noted some obstacles to listening on Monday when looking at the causes of conflict, but the key obstacles to listening relating to this chapter can be summarised as: a) the misconceptions that arise from the listener; and b) those that arise from external factors.

In another place
There is a big gap between the speed of speech and the speed of the mind. As a result we are tempted to listen but at the same time try to formulate clever questions or to visit our favourite dreamland.

Self-centred
We are so pre-occupied with our solution to the problem or

our view of the conflict issues that we do not *really* hear what is being said.

Hearing what you want to hear
We have our own agenda and nothing much else matters. It is the obverse of the old speaker's joke. 'I tell them everything three times, the first time they do not hear, the second time it enters their subconscious and after the third time they applaud – because I think the same way that they do!'

Listening with a script
We listen for facts or opinions that will later prove our point. In this mode we will also misinterpret the message.

External distraction
There are a wide variety of external distractions that can act as obstacles to our listening. They include background noise, uncomfortable seating or visual distractions. One of the most common is presenters who use highly detailed overhead slides that nobody can read.

Communication style
Many speakers have strong regional accents or use gestures to such an extent that the hassle to the listener prevents comprehension of the message.

Preconception
A two-way obstacle to listening and a source of conflict. The listener may have had a preview of what the other party is intending and so will not hear what is said or interpret to suit the preconception. And again the speaker may choose words for the same reason but based on their preconception. Though perhaps an extreme in business terms we can

observe the dangers of preconception in many of the racial and ethnic conflicts that dominate today's world.

However, we are influenced by third parties and cultural imperatives in our daily workplace. We have already noted the divisions between management and labour but there are others in which misconceptions can damage our ability to hear.

Summary

Today we have examined the power of listening as a tool to help us understand ourselves and to understand others. Good listening is at the heart of communication, and communication is at the heart of collaboration. In conclusion, we need to develop an environment in which all have eyes to see, ears to hear and the sense to feel.

Tomorrow we will turn our attention to resolving conflict.

Resolving conflict

Traditionally in business, opposing sides have resolved conflict in one of two ways: an imposed solution by one side or some form of compromise. Today, business is increasingly looking for a third way and this is particularly true in internal disputes which sap so much energy from an organisation.

An imposed solution is a situation in which one side gets just about everything it wants while the other side may get nothing. This type of solution may apply to both conflict between great corporations and conflict between management and labour within an organisation. In the corporate arena this usually happens when one competitor achieves an overwhelming power, through market position or financial clout. For example, the US Department of Justice considers that Microsoft has acted in that mode in the technology market. In the arena of trade union versus management disputes many examples could be cited on both sides but perhaps the most relevant in recent times was the conflict between Margaret Thatcher's government and the coal miners in the mid-80s.

The compromise position is usually better than the imposed solution but it tends to leave both sides unsatisfied. The resultant frustration can lead both sides to find an opportunity to score off the other later.

In truth compromise means that the two sides to the conflict are relatively equal in their ability to wield power to their own ends. In that situation each side gives up something else it values in order to hold on to something that it wants even more. In reality neither side gets everything it wants.

But both compromise and imposed solutions are often based on misconceptions about what the other party really wants or perhaps more important, what is really available. Bob Lapin, a leading USA management consultant based in Chicago, explains the issue in a simple way. You are at home and your two children come running to you with one orange that each wants. What do you do? At first glance, the compromise solution is to split the orange between the children. But this compromise is not the most effective result in the terms of conflict resolution. So instead you ask the question 'Why do you want the orange?' We now listen with empathy.

The first child responds that mummy has said that he must take more vitamin C or he will go down with scurvy. Now external power has been invoked but the second child must have her say and she explains that she is baking a cake for mummy and daddy and needs the orange peel for the icing. Our intrepid parent armed with the knowledge of the third way provides arbitration and rules that one has the peel and the other the fruit. In other words understanding the interest of others in an environment of mutual concern is the essence of conflict resolution.

The third way
There is a win-win alternative to imposition or compromise. A way of resolving conflict in which both sides are content with the outcome so both can consider that 'we have won!' In a win-win solution both sides aren't just mollified they are actually pleased because they have got what they really needed. This leaves both parties in a positive frame of mind with each other and trust between each has been enhanced. Now they look forward to increasing co-operation in the future. But, in truth, the win-win resolution of inter-company

conflict is still unusual because corporations and people are not environmentally trained to approach conflict in this way.

To some extent we covered this alternative approach for the company as a whole when we considered ADR on Tuesday. Today we will now concentrate on conflict within the organisation. Without always recognising it most companies have an operating culture based on individuals and competition. This is particularly so since the advent of the knowledge worker and self determined teams. Individualism and competition are in conflict with the methods used for conflict resolution. However, we must overcome these difficulties because constructive resolution of conflict is vital to the business. We need to learn how to disagree over issues but to persist until we come up with a solution to the benefit of all parties. We have to learn and practice the straightforward steps involved in resolving conflict.

The following steps will assist managers and employees to engage in productive conflict resolution:

- nullify emotion
- explore the reasons for conflict
- consider alternative solutions
- agree on the most appropriate
- implement the chosen solution
- evaluate the solution at work.

Nullify emotion

If strong emotions are evident on either side when an issue needs to be resolved, they must be nullified before proceeding. The same is true should it crop up in the heat of the moment: stop until it has subsided. Emotions can inhibit or distort communication which is critical to resolving dispute. The discussion can be postponed or just delayed for a short time. On resuming, the parties must feel free to find out why there are such strong emotions involved in the issue. This is not easy because with the nature of emotions they are not always eliminated by reasoned argument. Sometimes third party mediation will be needed.

Explore the reasons for conflict

Each party in any disagreement must be willing to discuss their view of the situation and then be willing to explore the other person's perception of the issue. Active listening by all parties is necessary to both hear what each is saying and to understand the facts and possible emotions that lie behind the disagreement.

Individual perceptions should not be criticised. Each person

should try to remain as objective as possible and so remain open to the views of others.

The whole purpose of the discussion is to determine the specific reasons for disagreement. As well as the objective facts the following questions need to be answered:

- are there any misconceptions about the issue?
- have the objectives of the parties been misinterpreted?
- are cultural or value issues involved?
- are there any personality conflicts?
- is resistance to change involved?

Consider alternative solutions

Usually disputes in business are about differing views of a course of action to be taken. If we have nullified emotion and discussed all the issues around the dispute we are now in the frame of mind to examine the alternative solutions.

Each party to the dispute must now have the opportunity and the time to fully describe their proposed solution. All possible solutions must be considered and the reasons why each solution might be appropriate should be explored. If the appropriate solution is not immediately obvious and accepted by all parties there should be a pause before moving to another step. A time for reflection on the discussions can have a positive effect on the issue.

Agreement on the appropriate solution

The parties need to agree on the appropriate solution to allow the business processes involved to continue effectively.

If no agreement has been reached after either consideration of the competing solutions or a short time for reflection, other techniques may be necessary.

Either party could call for negotiation if they feel that it could help to resolve the impasse. This gives each party an opportunity to modify their preferred solutions or to develop another solution altogether. Negotiation involves giving and taking and enables parties in conflict to collaborate on finding a solution. Two other books in this series develop this concept in more detail – *Successful Negotiating* and *Successfully Dealing with Difficult People*.

If all of these efforts have still failed a neutral third party (another manager or specialist in the process involved) may be brought in to arbitrate and resolve the disagreement. The worst solution is to make no decision on the appropriate solution. Apart from the impact on the performance of the business process involved, the disagreement between the parties will continue to simmer and fester. This will impair effective working relationships and sooner or later will re-emerge in a new and more emotionally charged conflict. Unresolved conflicts can become a deadly cancer in any organisation.

Implement the chosen solution

If we have reached this stage we are generally discussing an improvement or change to an existing work process or activity. Successful implementation of the new solution will depend on two things. These are:

- support from management and process stakeholders

- an organised plan for implementation with realistic, understood and actionable goals.

People tend not to like change, especially change that on the surface appears to be inconvenient. To ensure the success of the chosen solution it is imperative to communicate to all involved the reasons for the choice of solution and the improved performance from the change throughout the duration of implementation. Highlight implementation goals and progress against them.

A sense of being involved is one of the great motivators in business, so communication of goals and achievement are essential to success.

Evaluate the solution

A constant source of frustration and conflict in business is a management tendency to launch some new initiative or to implement a new approach to a business process . . . and then walk away. In management's eyes they have supported the implementation of a new approach and now they must turn their minds to the next problem. Those involved with the change or the agreed solution to the agreement perceive new priorities and decide to let sleeping dogs lie. The overall result is that nobody really evaluates the new solution or finds out if it is solving the conflict and improving performance.

For continuous performance improvement (the only real reason for all this concern about conflict) it is vital to evaluate the effectiveness of every change or solution to conflict. If the new process is failing we need to determine what is causing the failure and devise another or amended solution.

The implementation plan should define the measuring and auditing of the solution as it is implemented. Failure is in essence another conflict to be resolved and so the whole process must begin again.

Management's role

It is management's responsibility to establish a purpose, focus and values for the organisation they lead. These areas combine to establish the culture of an organisation so they must be continually revisited and, if necessary, updated to meet the prevailing technology or marketing challenge. Conflict resolution is one of the keys to modern business so it is imperative on management to fit their organisation to properly manage conflict.

First management needs to understand that conflict is natural and cannot be eliminated by decree. Indeed they need to nurture constructive conflict dedicated to finding new solutions, new products, new services and a new understanding of the marketplace.

In many organisations conflict, controversy and dispute are discouraged by managers who want to maintain the status quo or our 'caring culture'. Such thinking is dangerous and will only lead to the ultimate decline of the organisation which is surrendering to complacency and sheer laziness. Only when people are allowed to draw out and value different points of view and discuss them in an open atmosphere will conflict be seen as an essential element for success.

To achieve this vibrant culture management must recognise that conflict will never be resolved constructively by accident. Management's role is to ensure that all members of the organisation are taught and encouraged to understand and continuously practice with the techniques of conflict resolution. We will consider the implications of this approach on Friday and Saturday.

Summary

Today we have considered different approaches to resolving conflict. These alternatives included imposition, compromise and collaboration. The third way involved some difficult techniques in terms of human emotions and reactions but was demonstrated to be the only win-win solution. We concluded today's discussion considering the role of management in creating a culture for resolving conflict.

We have now set the scene for discussing Friday's subject – 'the collaborative culture'.

The collaborative culture

A whole new attitude to employment and the development of people is required for modern business. Management must recognise that the more the demand rises for skilled people, the more those people will in turn demand a share in determining or at least influencing their own destiny.

Leading companies are already demonstrating that open communication, empowerment and the education and training of their people are decisive factors in their success. The corporation that forms a collaborative partnership with its people releases massive potential for the good of both the company and its customers.

The changing workplace

The convergence of technologies, the growing proportion of knowledge workers, and the evolution of rising expectations are themselves converging to have a profound effect on the workplace. In particular, the traditional relationship between the employer and the employee is changing dramatically. However, like most evolutions it takes longer than expected for new patterns of employment to become general.

The world of work is currently in the first stage of this evolution. Some companies are way ahead and are developing their personnel policies and people for later stages. Now the traditional pyramid is disappearing, to be replaced with a 'bag of marbles' – a collection of interdependent units continuously changing their personnel and relationships to tackle project after project. The corporate objective is to co-ordinate and to communicate effectively with the 'white spot' on the marbles, to create a cohesive collaborative culture.

In this culture employers and employees are working together in seeking win-win solutions to meeting the demands of the customer focused global market. It is interesting that change so often takes us back to where we once were. Conceptually the move towards the independent – contractor knowledge worker is not unlike the relationship of the individual craftsman to the merchant prior to the industrial revolution.

New attitudes

In a collaborative culture, talented and assiduous workers will view this as an opportunity to define and control their destinies in line with their complete life aspirations: freedom to choose when they want to work and with whom; and freedom to manage their own time, thus taking full account of social aspirations such as family and outside interests. The level of wealth for a large number of people is determined by their own decisions on the balance of choice between work and play. Business needs to remember that these are growing attitudes amongst the best educated and trained employees, sought by most leading companies.

From the point of view of the corporation, a collaborative culture provides massive opportunities to provide a flexible response to every situation it faces in an evolving marketplace. The classic inertia of the corporate heavyweight can be replaced with the fast footwork and rapid punching of the flyweight boxer.

Employee focus

The primary focus of an organisation should be on the customer but that cannot be sustained unless there is also a company focus on the employee. The best companies are beginning to see employees as their internal customers, who also have needs and expectations. They recognise that employees have valuable knowledge of what is *really happening* in the organisation.

Successful communication between management and employees can forge a collaborative culture in delighting customers. Yet too often management and employees act as adversaries, with customers the victims of the conflict. Even enlightened management can fall into the trap of communicating *at* rather than *with* employees. This is because management usually sets the agenda.

For a really collaborative culture, management must provide the means and the *permission* for employees to set some agendas of their own. Business needs open communication systems that allow speedy communication from workers about the problems they are currently facing or anticipating – problems that interfere with the objective of delighting customers.

Cultural assessment

The culture of an organisation is assessed from the day-to-day actions and behaviour of its members. These are governed by the real value systems, which are not necessarily those written down or expressed by its leaders. The environment is thus based on the perceptions that drive the actions of those involved, and these can be in direct conflict with stated values. Organisational culture is established by how management acts rather than by what it says.

The development of a collaborative culture should therefore start with some form of assessment of both the real culture and barriers that might exist to constructive dispute resolution. For our purposes we do not need a full employee survey or other highly detailed data. At this stage we are assessing people's perceptions of the issues surrounding a collaborative culture and if there is a need to change the existing culture.

Perceptions

We all have perceptions about how our organisation works and may find that our perceptions differ from those of colleagues in other departments or at other levels. Our opinions have been built up by our day-to-day experiences. In time, we all tend to make decisions or behave towards one another on the basis of our individual perceptions. In this way perceptions become self-prophesising elements that make up the culture.

Questioning

Assessment is about questioning, so we begin by interviewing managers and other employees at key locations in the organisation. The number and selection of interviewees will differ in every organisation but a representative sample which includes key functions, levels, gender and ethnic minorities is the model.

Initially, we are looking at the overall collaborative culture within the organisation. Later we consider how we handle dispute with outside bodies. Therefore our early questions are targeted at interpersonal conflict resolution.

Typical questions to which we want answers include:

- are dispute resolution methods familiar to all the workforce?
- are dispute resolution methods perceived to be fair and effective and trusted by employees not to result in retaliation?
- are potential conflict situations (instances of harassment, discriminations or unfairness) viewed as harmful and discouraged?
- are interpersonal skills encouraged and considered important for job success?

As part of the assessment, some broader questions should be asked of managers relating to the environment for fostering constructive conflict. Interestingly, a negative answer may plant a seed in fertile ground for a need to know as well as making those questioned more receptive to any future initiative to foster a collaborative culture:

- Are process models, problem solving and statistical process control (SPC) methodology widely used?

These are the essential tools of work process management and the continuous communication about ways to improve production, marketing and administration. These methods are described in detail in another book in this series – *Understanding Total Quality Management*.

- Is purposeful teamwork, involving cross-functional or departmental members, a normal way of working?

Teamwork is the basis for a whole new way of collaborative

working toward delighting customers and gaining competitive advantage. Unfortunately the concept has been prostituted in many companies so that teams just add to the proliferation of meetings and wasted time. Teams are only productive if they are brought together for a specific purpose and disbanded once the purpose has been achieved or resolved.

- Are the concepts of knowledge management understood and utilised?

Knowledge management is the process of making creative, effective and efficient use of all the knowledge and information available to an organisation for the benefit of its customers and thus the company. Another book in this series, *Understanding Knowledge Management*, describes the process in detail.

- Are briefings on future technology, market and business trends a regular feature for employees?

They spur ideas and constructive conflict. Anticipating the future helps to eliminate future business shocks.

External collaboration

Our organisation does not exist in a vacuum. There are many external groups, companies or bodies on whom we depend or who could be a source of conflict. A collaborative culture will ensure that some are involved in the family. In other words, our communication with outside bodies is an essential element in our culture. As part of our assessment the last group of questions we want answered are as follows:

- Is the principal focus of the company on its customers?

Communicating with customers has to be a considered, planned and organised activity. Too often, management is satisfied only with the quick fix solution of customer care training for receptionists and others who talk directly with customers so that they are courteous and caring.

- Are suppliers considered an extension of the business?

We should be in constant positive communication with our suppliers so that they are involved with us in a partnership of interest. Too many companies treat their suppliers as an opponent to be squeezed for the last penny. Constructive conflict about processes and each other's capabilities can expand the potential for both.

- Does our organisation have a constructive relationship with regulatory bodies?

Every organisation is constrained or protected by various regulations that usually emanate from some form of public authority or professional body. For many companies this is all viewed as costly red tape holding back the business and as a result the regulatory bodies are soon regarded as combatants to be destroyed or at least hoodwinked. This attitude can create a destructive environment as, for example, British Nuclear Fuels recently found to their cost. Collaboration can often ameliorate or provide advance notice of regulations or even spark innovative solutions.

> • Does our organisation communicate effectively with special interest groups and the community at large?

Many organisations are in a reactive mode to such groups and are therefore caught out in angry disputes carried out in the glare of media publicity. As with all communication issues in business, handling the media and crisis confrontation need prior thought and planning. You may not be able to anticipate the exact nature of a crisis, but you can plan crisis management in communications.

Active involvement in the community, as opposed to the passive option of 'sending a cheque', is becoming an important issue in the marketplace. Companies are now conscious that a collaborative reputation in the community will help them.

Assessment findings

The findings of the cultural assessment should be presented to senior management. This is likely to provoke lively discussion, which was of course the point of the assessment. The results are likely to include:

• A wide divergence of individual perceptions of the real

state of collaboration in the organisation and with external bodies.
- A general recognition that barriers to collaboration do exist.
- A surprised recognition of the level of frustration and wasted potential involved in continual conflicts that are not resolved.
- An identification of some key areas for improvement.

Recognition and acceptance of need

The general reaction to this kind of assessment is, 'What are we going to do about it?' In other words there is a recognition and acceptance of the need to change. We will aim to answer that question on Saturday.

Summary

Today we have considered a collaborative culture and assessed the status of our organisation in relation to the ideal. In particular we looked at our relationship to:

- the changing workplace
- employee attitudes
- people's perceptions
- our stance to interpersonal conflict
- our use of collaborative tools and concepts
- external relationships.

Tomorrow we will discuss the issues involved in implementing a cultural change and how to help our people to get involved.

Helping the people

Yesterday our assessment helped us to recognise that we need to modify our management culture if we are to develop an environment that encourages collaborative ways to resolve conflict. However, we cannot change our overall organisational culture without changing management behaviour.

Later today we will consider how to plan for and launch a series of actions that will achieve our aim but perhaps first we should take some measurement of how our managers are behaving.

Test your managerial temperature

An article in the journal *Professional Manager* (March 2000) provided an interesting questionnaire for the measurement of management performance in this area. Written by Keith Ovenden and Ian Pitchford of Top flight Training Ltd, it suggested that managers should guage their temperatures as managers as either 'hot or cold or just a bit frosty'.

The reader may enjoy taking this modified test and mark themselves on a sliding scale from 5 (hot) down to 0 for cold, negative managers. There are ten questions:

1. *Do you encourage personnel at all levels to input their ideas and thoughts about how the working environment processes and policies can be improved?*

0	1	2	3	4	5

Structured meetings or briefings provide opportunities at all levels for input. Feedback is essential for building self-esteem, confidence, loyalty and trust.

2. *Do you deal with disputes or grievances as they occur?*

0	1	2	3	4	5

Festering disputes will lower morale and destroy an open door policy.

3. *Do you look on mistakes as learning opportunities?*

0	1	2	3	4	5

Open and honest evaluation of mistakes will assist in identifying areas for improvement. Encourage an attitude of 'could we have done this better'. Witch-hunts bring the cancer of fear into the organisation.

4. *Do you share information with your team?*

0	1	2	3	4	5

People will accept difficult situations more readily if they are properly informed or 'kept in the picture'. The 'need to know syndrome' is often an abuse of power.

5. *Do you encourage a climate of continuous personal development?*

0	1	2	3	4	5

Effective training that addresses the needs of both the organisation and the individual will release potential. Education and training should be seen as an investment not as an on-cost.

6. *Do you foster a positive praise culture that recognises and rewards effort?*

0	1	2	3	4	5

A simple thank you goes a long way towards developing trust and collaboration.

7. *Do you ensure that the standards expected of employees are clearly communicated?*

0	1	2	3	4	5

Make the standards clear and strive to maintain them yourself. Employees actually do not respect too 'easy' managers; they expect high standards from their leader.

8. *Are you well organised, particularly with regard to managing meetings?*

0	1	2	3	4	5

This is the achilles heel of so many managers. Meetings should be well structured, minuted, with clear agendas and run to a declared timescale. One of the most immediate ways to make an impact as a manager.

9. *Do all your employees have the necessary resources to achieve the tasks set them?*

0	1	2	3	4	5

Inadequate resources is the most usual source of conflict in modern organisations. The real need to reduce costs is often addressed by a uniform reduction of budgets with little reference to the work processes. Managers need to fight for realistic budgets to achieve their objectives or openly reduce the output of their processes. There is a limit to the stress that employees will endure to protect their jobs.

10. *Do you regularly ask yourself 'Am I fulfilling my responsibilities as a manager'?*

0	1	2	3	4	5

The role of the manager is to help their people achieve the corporate objectives and to maximise their potential. The manager does not have to be expert at everything.

Check your temperature:

40–50	You're really hot stuff – but if you cheated you should be pink with embarrassment
30–39	Warm hearted and generous
20–29	Warming to the job
10–19	Apply for the next management development course
0–9	Resign or defrost immediately

Planning to change

A management team to represent all the elements of the organisation should be selected to prepare a plan to develop our collaborative culture. Their task can be summarised as follows:

- To develop a purpose statement and set of collaborative values to be communicated to the whole organisation
- To develop the education and training for all managers and employees to enable them
- To develop supporting actions.

Purpose and values

People will respond to leadership which involves them in the objective. In a business organisation the leadership must be initiated by the senior executives and then be fully supported by the managers who have direct contact with the employees. It is not enough to make an executive announcement and then place beautifully framed mission statements in the foyer and in the canteen, and then expect the culture to change.

Executives must develop clear purpose statements of their commitment to the values of a collaborative culture. They then demonstrate that commitment by ensuring that all managers are trained as to how their actions will implement the new culture. In other words managers must begin to practice the values before they call on employee commitment.

Employees are not idiots and will quickly respond to a change of behaviour in their managers. Of course there will be some sceptical reactions because of past experience with management initiatives of a new 'flavour of the month'. They will soon raise or instigate conflict situations to test that the newly proclaimed culture is for real.

Clearly culture change is not a quick one-off event. It will take time and perseverance so management involvement and support is a continuous process of collaborating with employees.

Creativity and trust

Constructive collaboration will only take place if the values and methods employed are credible throughout the organisation. Trust is the prime value for a collaborative culture. In that environment people tend to trust one another which leads to openness about disagreement and possible future conflict. Erik van Slyke lists seven characteristics of trustworthy people which, with this author's explanation, are as follows:

- *courtesy*: they show respect for the other person's viewpoint and time requirements – they give uninterrupted attention to what they say
- *composure*: they demonstrate confidence and self awareness
- *sincerity*: they mean what they say and believe in the power of collaboration
- *integrity*: they seek the best solution and so they are prepared to admit their own weaknesses and mistakes, but expect the same from the other party
- *fairness*: they are objective and use facts and information as a basis for sound and logical reasoning – they control their emotions
- *reliability*: they follow through on their commitments and convey the whole picture to their colleagues
- *competence*: they prepare for meetings and understand the tools of collaborative discussion and the relevant facts about the dispute.

Education and training

The most powerful vehicle available to executives to build a collaborative partnership with their people is education and training. There is a difference. In business, we want to influence employee attitudes so that they take common ownership of the collaborative culture. Education also gives employees the confidence to think for themselves within the horizon of the conflict resolution values. Training is directed toward competence in the systems and techniques for conflict resolution. In this context managing change is a core competency for managers.

Adult learning in business is most effective when it directly

relates to the workplace. Employees at all levels are more likely to understand and retain knowledge if they have an easy transition with practice of the new concepts in their own work.

| THEORY | → | PRACTICE | → | ACTION |

In such an environment, in-house instructors are more effective than external specialists. Preferably, the in-house instructors are also fellow managers or knowledge workers rather than professional trainers from the education department. To some extent this is governed by the subject and the existing level of knowledge and participatory experience within the organisation. But it does indicate that an important element in management development should be teaching mechanics. Managers need to continuously acquire knowledge but they should also commit to sharing knowledge.

The purpose of the educational element is to ensure ownership of the new collaborative culture. In other words we are aiming to change or develop attitudes in the behaviour of the people in the organisation. It's an appeal through hearts and minds for a positive constructive approach.

The purpose of the training element is more obvious but equally important. It is to provide the competence in communication, in listening, in analysis and all the techniques of conflict resolution.

Initial objectives

The initial objectives of the process to implement a collaborative culture mostly relate to people's behaviour. They can be summarised as follows:

- Ensure that managers and employees are aware of the alternative ways to resolve conflict and the organisation's need to employ them. These will include collaboration, mediation, negotiation and arbitration and operational techniques for process modelling and problem solving.
- Managers help employees to handle interpersonal conflict in positive ways and eliminate anti-social behaviour in the workplace. They must ensure that resentment, envy and hidden personal agendas are not appreciated.
- Managers should be encouraging employees to share and transfer knowledge of problems and their resolution to help others.
- The organisation's plan should define three key work processes in obvious need of improvement and whose

resolution will make a significant contribution to performance.
- There should be continuous communication about the successes and the overall progress of the cultural revolution.

Audit and re-affirmation

The original plan to implement a process of collaboration should have defined the key objectives and the measures to accord success. An audit body should be established to continuously monitor progress and help corrective action if necessary.

At appropriate times the executives and senior managers should re-affirm the organisation's continuous commitment to the process. They should be alert to the fact that employees measure commitment to a cause by actions rather than words.

Summary

Today we have examined some elements in planning for and establishing a collaborative culture. We recognised the importance of the following:

- management have the responsibility to make it happen
- careful planning is essential
- consistent purpose and values supported by management are key
- establish trust and encourage creativity
- education and training
- management will be measured by actions rather than words.

CONCLUSION

Conflict in the workplace and between businesses *can* be managed effectively – and when resolved is a powerful contributor to a sustained competitive advantage.

NOTES

Further *Successful Business in a Week* titles from Hodder & Stoughton and the Institute of Management all at £6.99

All Hodder & Stoughton books are available from your local bookshop or can be ordered direct from the publisher. Just tick the titles you want and fill in the form below. Prices and availability subject to change without notice.

To: Hodder & Stoughton Ltd, Cash Sales Department, Bookpoint, 39 Milton Park, Abingdon, Oxon, OX14 4TD. If you have a credit card you may order by telephone – 01235 400414.
E-mail address: orders@bookpoint.co.uk
Please enclose a cheque or postal order made payable to Bookpoint Ltd to the value of the cover price and allow the following for postage and packaging:
UK & BFPO: £4.30 for one book; £6.30 for two books; £8.30 for three books.
OVERSEAS & EIRE: £4.80 for one book; £7.10 for 2 or 3 books (surface mail).

Name: ....

Address: ....

....

If you would prefer to pay by credit card, please complete:

Please debit my Visa/Mastercard/Diner's Card/American Express (delete as appropriate) card no:

❏ ❏ ❏ ❏ ❏ ❏ ❏ ❏ ❏ ❏ ❏ ❏ ❏ ❏ ❏ ❏

Signature .... Expiry Date ....